Thom Edison

SADDLEBACK
EDUCATIONAL PUBLISHING

Saddleback's Graphic Biographies

SADDLEBACK
EDUCATIONAL PUBLISHING
Three Watson
Irvine, CA 92618-2767
Website: www.sdlback.com

ISBN-13: 978-1-59905-228-1
ISBN-10: 1-59905-228-8
eBook: 978-1-60291-591-6

Printed in China

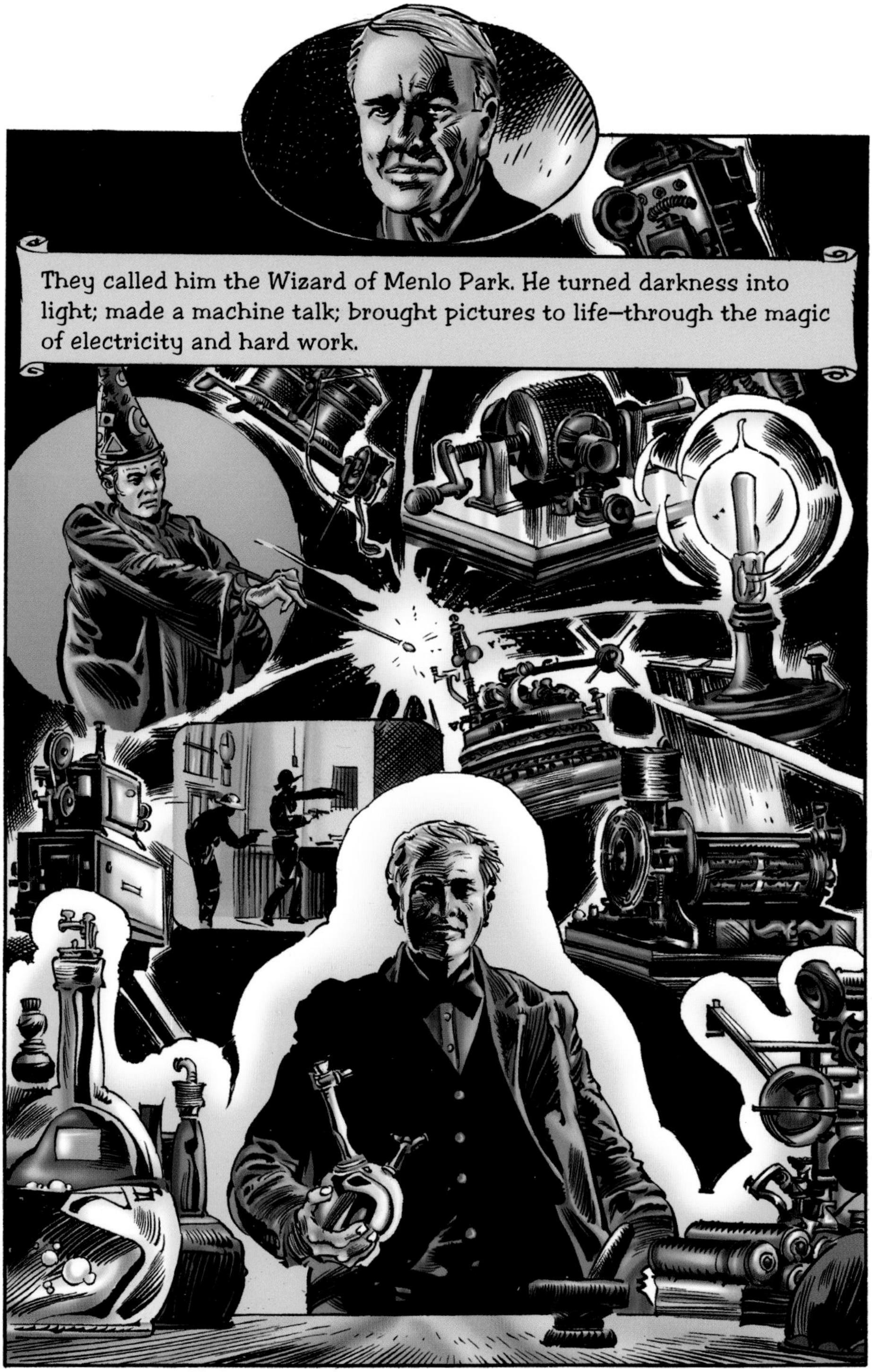
They called him the Wizard of Menlo Park. He turned darkness into light; made a machine talk; brought pictures to life—through the magic of electricity and hard work.

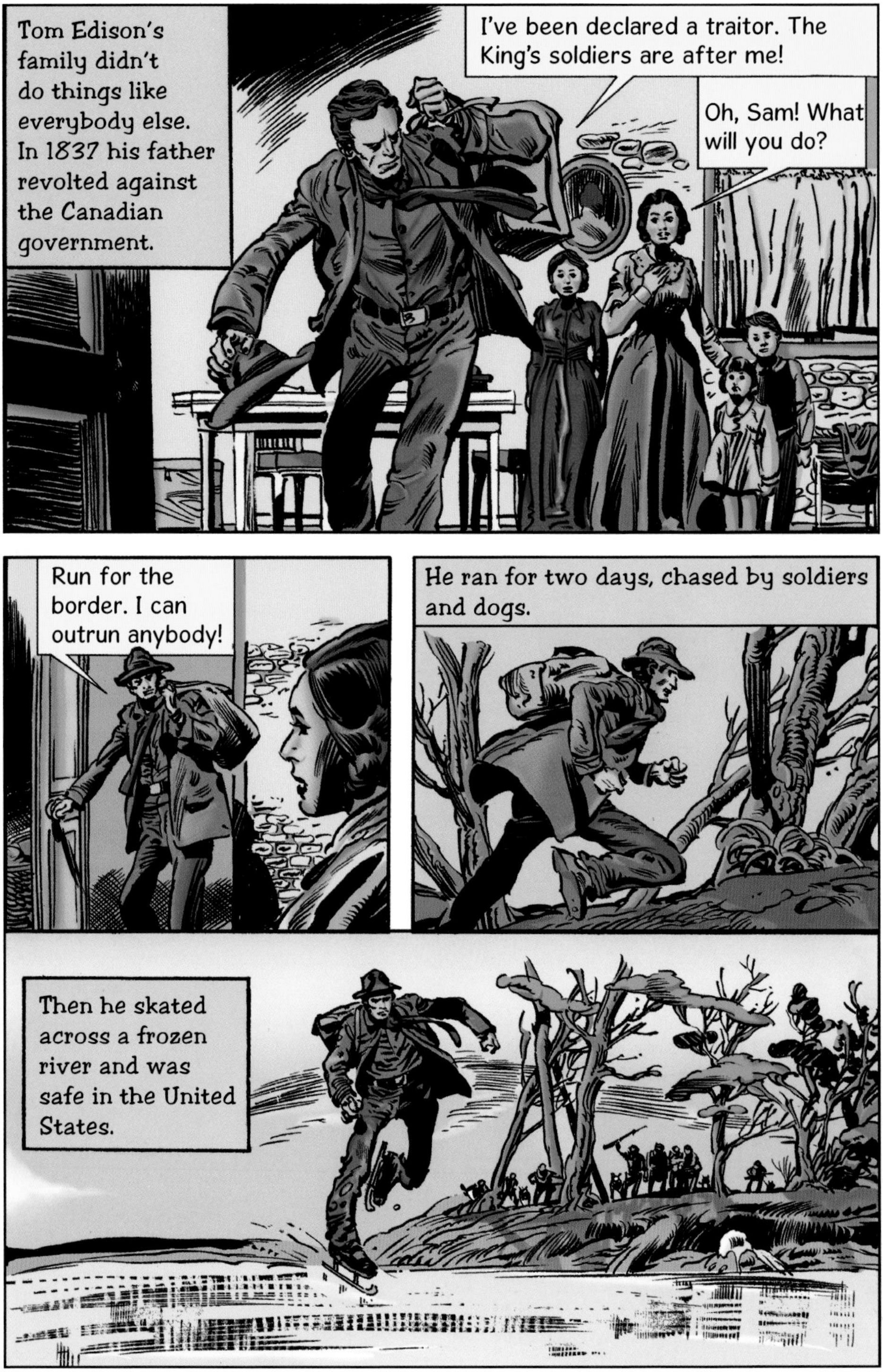
Tom Edison's family didn't do things like everybody else. In 1837 his father revolted against the Canadian government.
I've been declared a traitor. The King's soldiers are after me!
Oh, Sam! What will you do?
Run for the border. I can outrun anybody!
He ran for two days, chased by soldiers and dogs.
Then he skated across a frozen river and was safe in the United States.

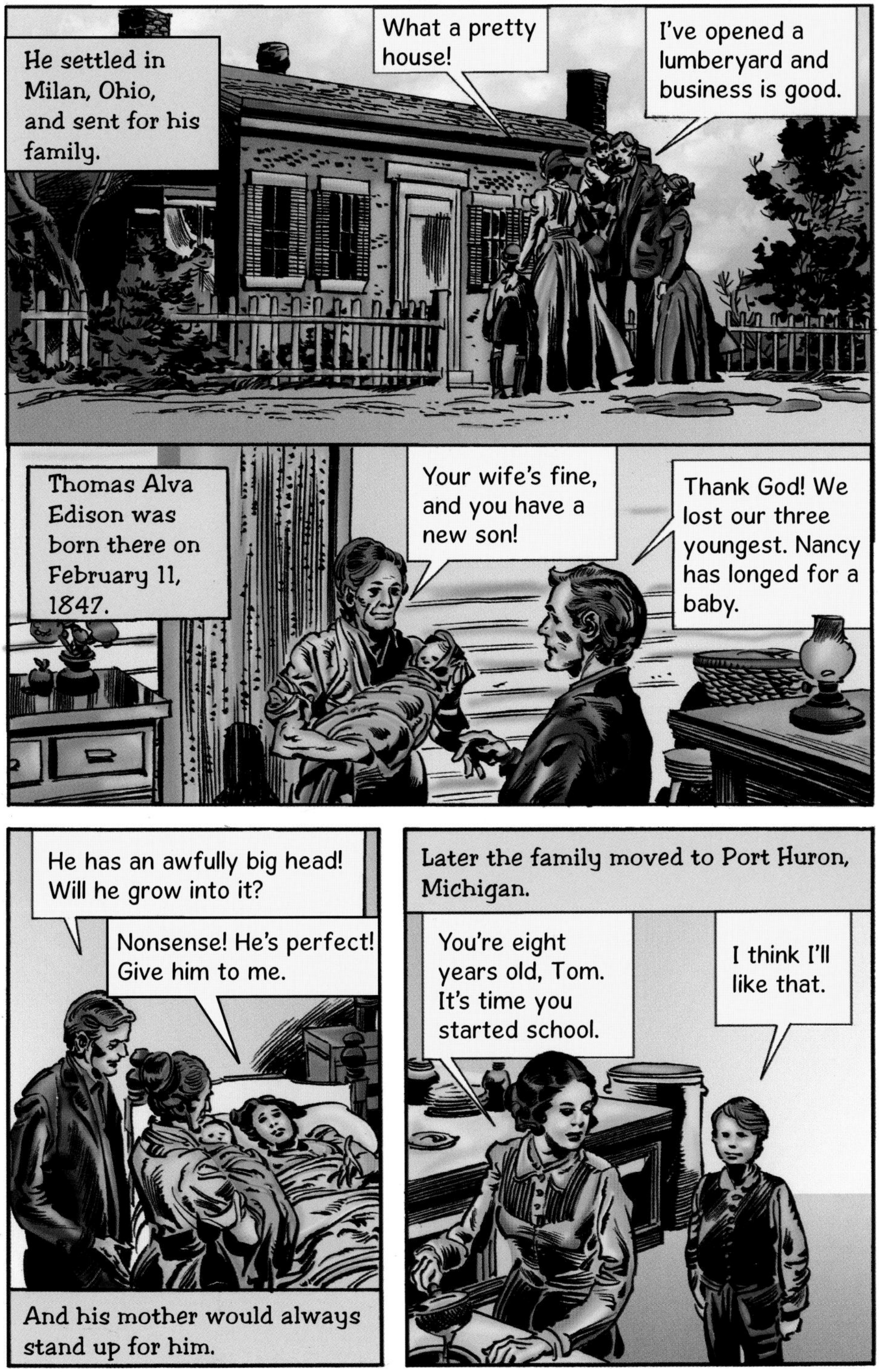
He settled in Milan, Ohio, and sent for his family.
What a pretty house!
I've opened a lumberyard and business is good.
Thomas Alva Edison was born there on February 11, 1847.
Your wife's fine, and you have a new son!
Thank God! We lost our three youngest. Nancy has longed for a baby.
He has an awfully big head! Will he grow into it?
Nonsense! He's perfect! Give him to me.
And his mother would always stand up for him.
Later the family moved to Port Huron, Michigan.
You're eight years old, Tom. It's time you started school.
I think I'll like that.

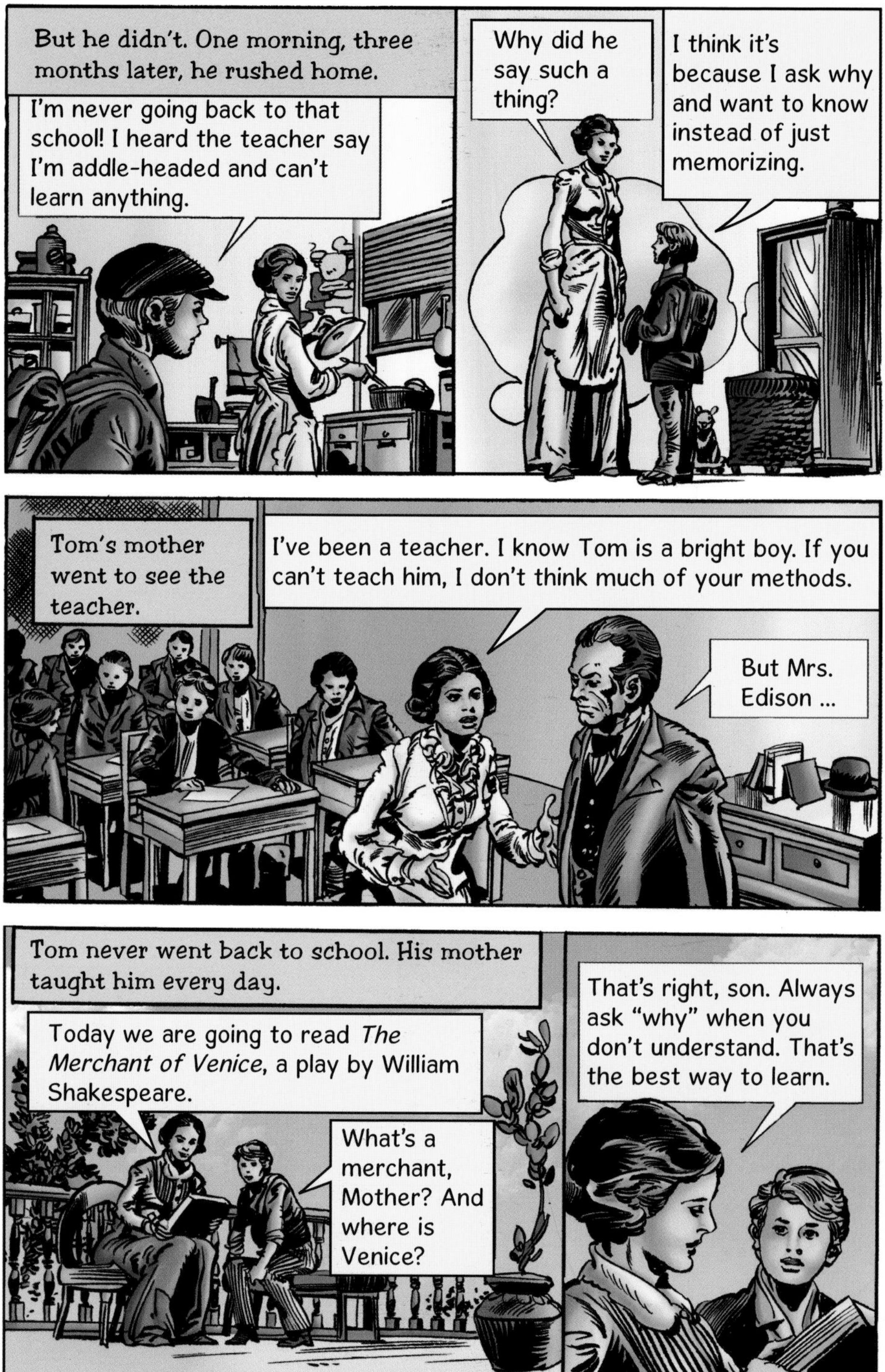

But he didn't. One morning, three months later, he rushed home.
I'm never going back to that school! I heard the teacher say I'm addle-headed and can't learn anything.
Why did he say such a thing?
I think it's because I ask why and want to know instead of just memorizing.
Tom's mother went to see the teacher.
I've been a teacher. I know Tom is a bright boy. If you can't teach him, I don't think much of your methods.
But Mrs. Edison ...
Tom never went back to school. His mother taught him every day.
Today we are going to read *The Merchant of Venice*, a play by William Shakespeare.
What's a merchant, Mother? And where is Venice?
That's right, son. Always ask "why" when you don't understand. That's the best way to learn.

I have a new book for you. Can you read the title?

And one day ...

D-I-C-T-I-O-N-A-R-Y Dictionary! *Dictionary of Science!*

He liked the new book.

I like science. I want to have a laboratory and mix things together to see what happens.

That is the science of chemistry.

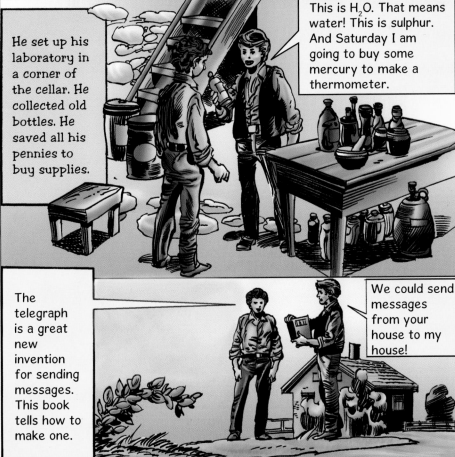

He set up his laboratory in a corner of the cellar. He collected old bottles. He saved all his pennies to buy supplies.

This is H_2O. That means water! This is sulphur. And Saturday I am going to buy some mercury to make a thermometer.

The telegraph is a great new invention for sending messages. This book tells how to make one.

We could send messages from your house to my house!

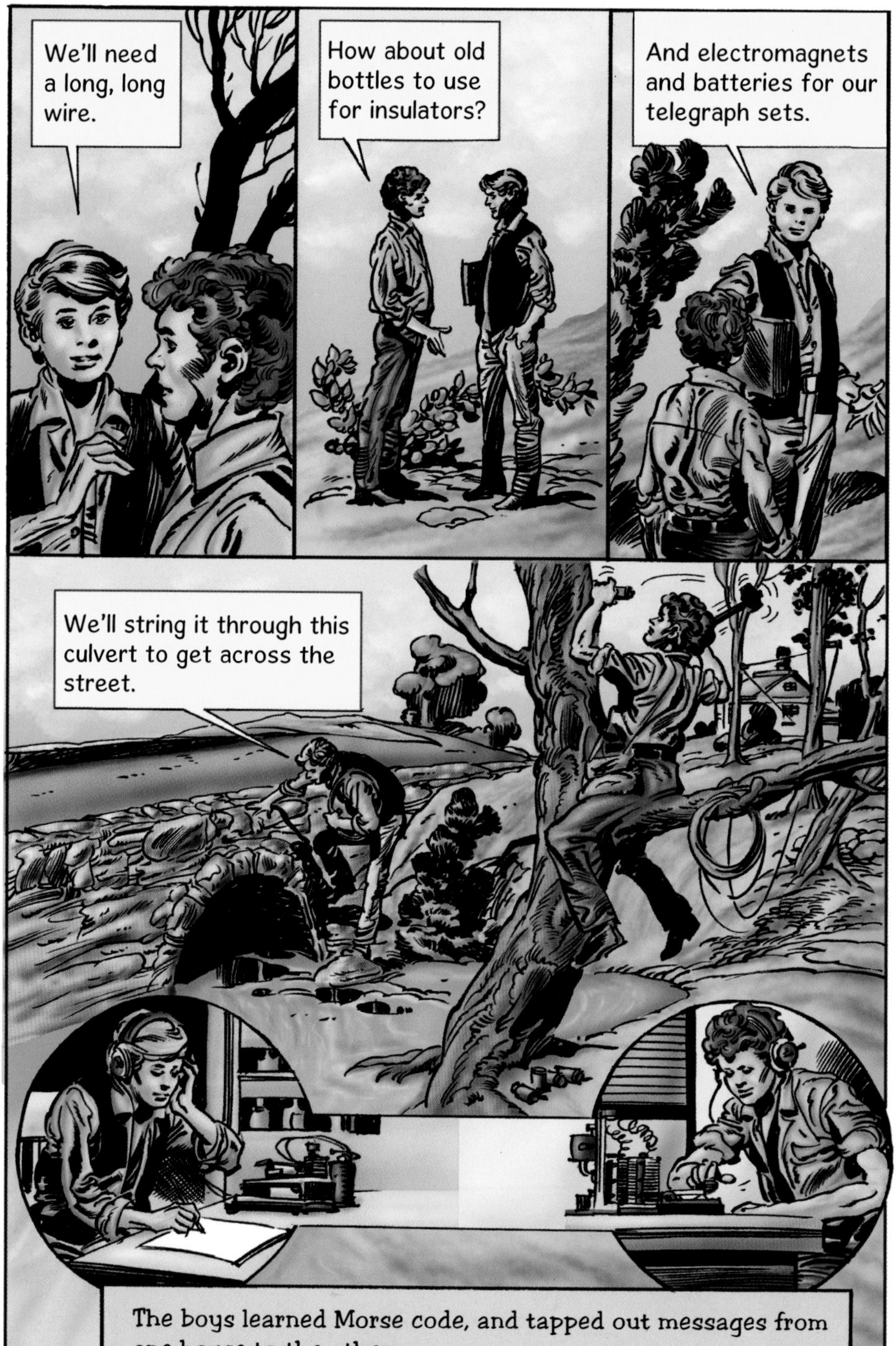
We'll need a long, long wire.
How about old bottles to use for insulators?
And electromagnets and batteries for our telegraph sets.
We'll string it through this culvert to get across the street.
The boys learned Morse code, and tapped out messages from one house to the other.

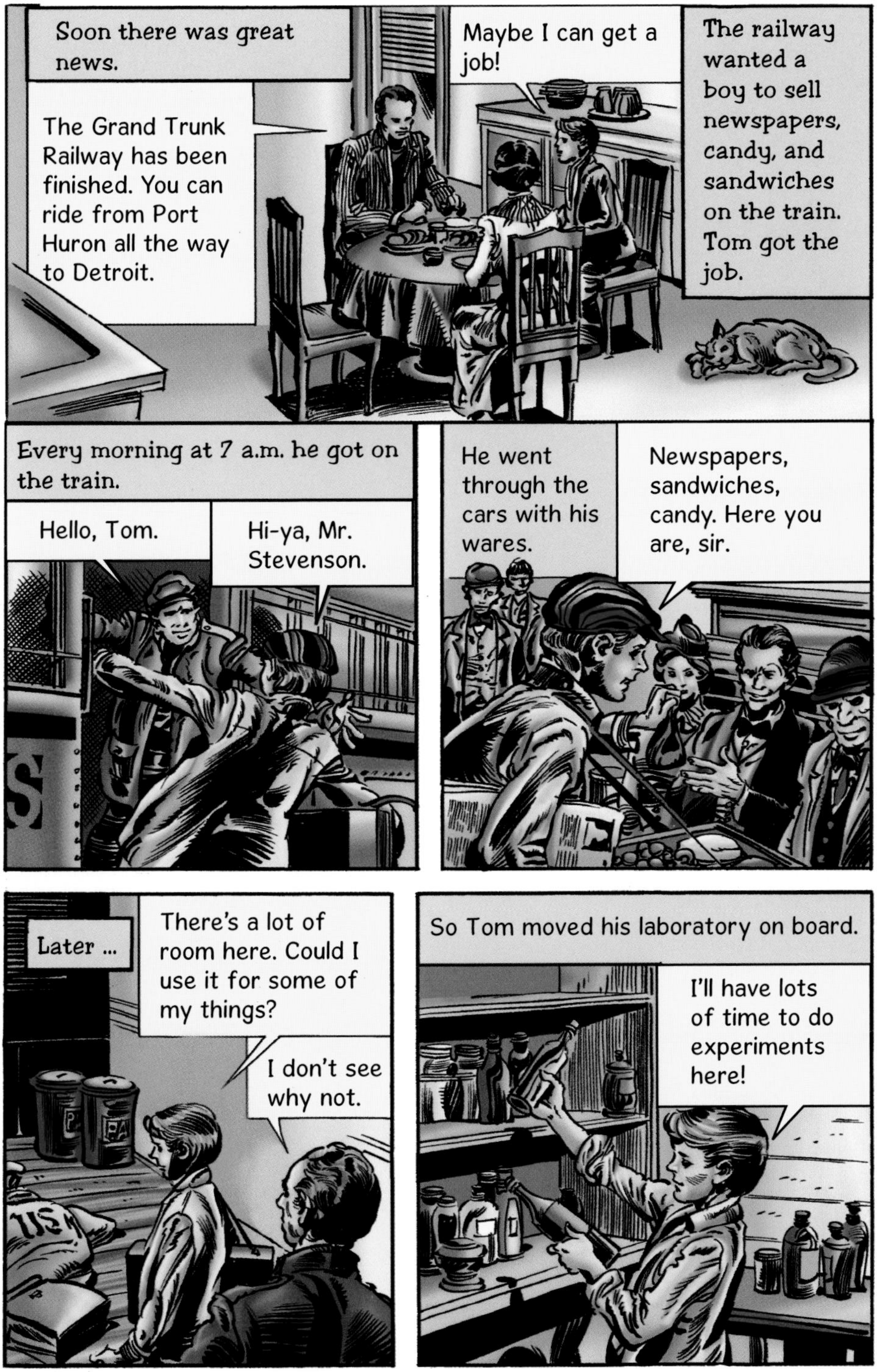
Soon there was great news.
The Grand Trunk Railway has been finished. You can ride from Port Huron all the way to Detroit.
Maybe I can get a job!
The railway wanted a boy to sell newspapers, candy, and sandwiches on the train. Tom got the job.
Every morning at 7 a.m. he got on the train.
Hello, Tom.
Hi-ya, Mr. Stevenson.
He went through the cars with his wares.
Newspapers, sandwiches, candy. Here you are, sir.
Later ...
There's a lot of room here. Could I use it for some of my things?
I don't see why not.
So Tom moved his laboratory on board.
I'll have lots of time to do experiments here!

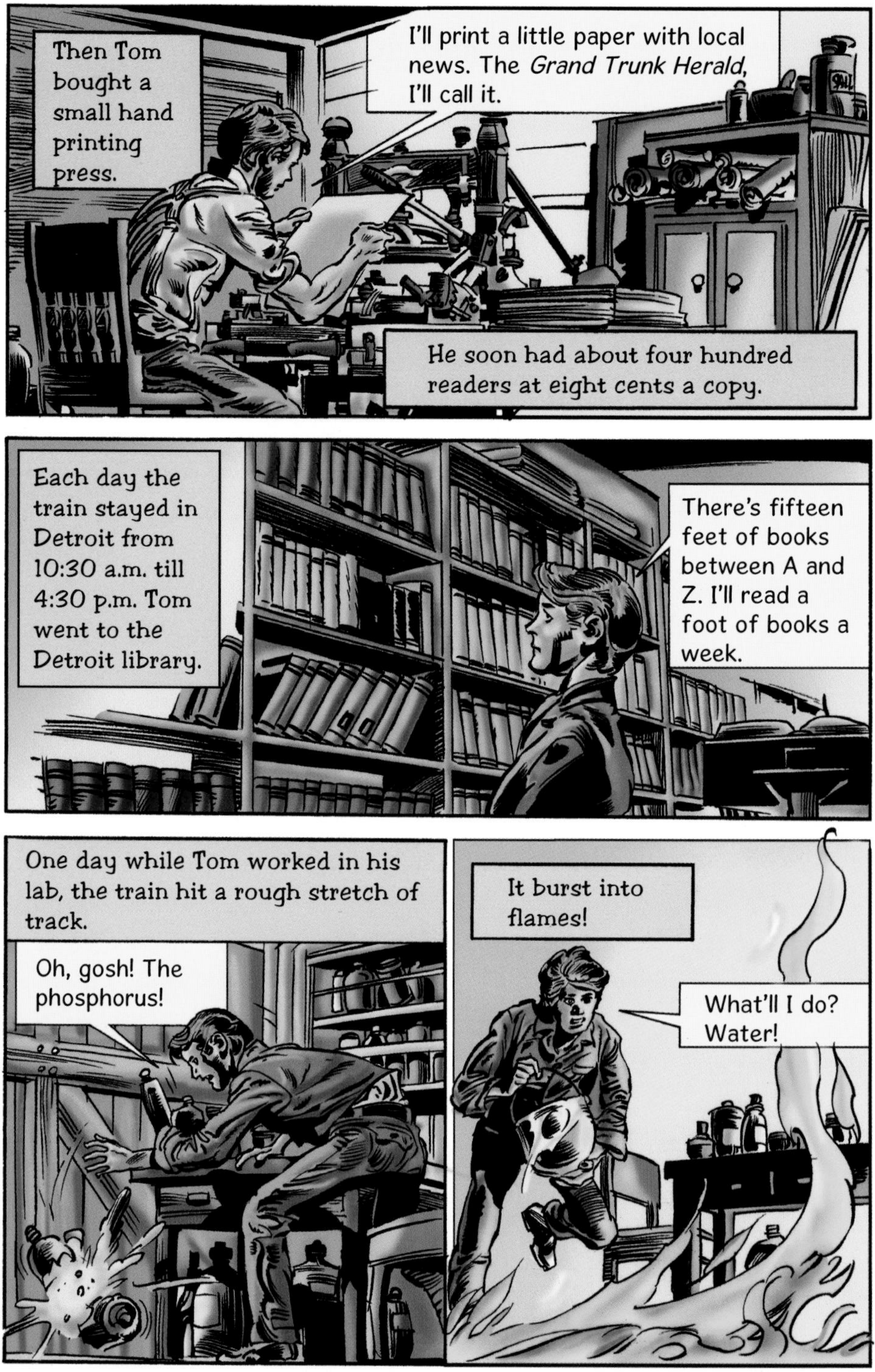
Then Tom bought a small hand printing press.
I'll print a little paper with local news. The *Grand Trunk Herald*, I'll call it.
He soon had about four hundred readers at eight cents a copy.
Each day the train stayed in Detroit from 10:30 a.m. till 4:30 p.m. Tom went to the Detroit library.
There's fifteen feet of books between A and Z. I'll read a foot of books a week.
One day while Tom worked in his lab, the train hit a rough stretch of track.
Oh, gosh! The phosphorus!
It burst into flames!
What'll I do? Water!

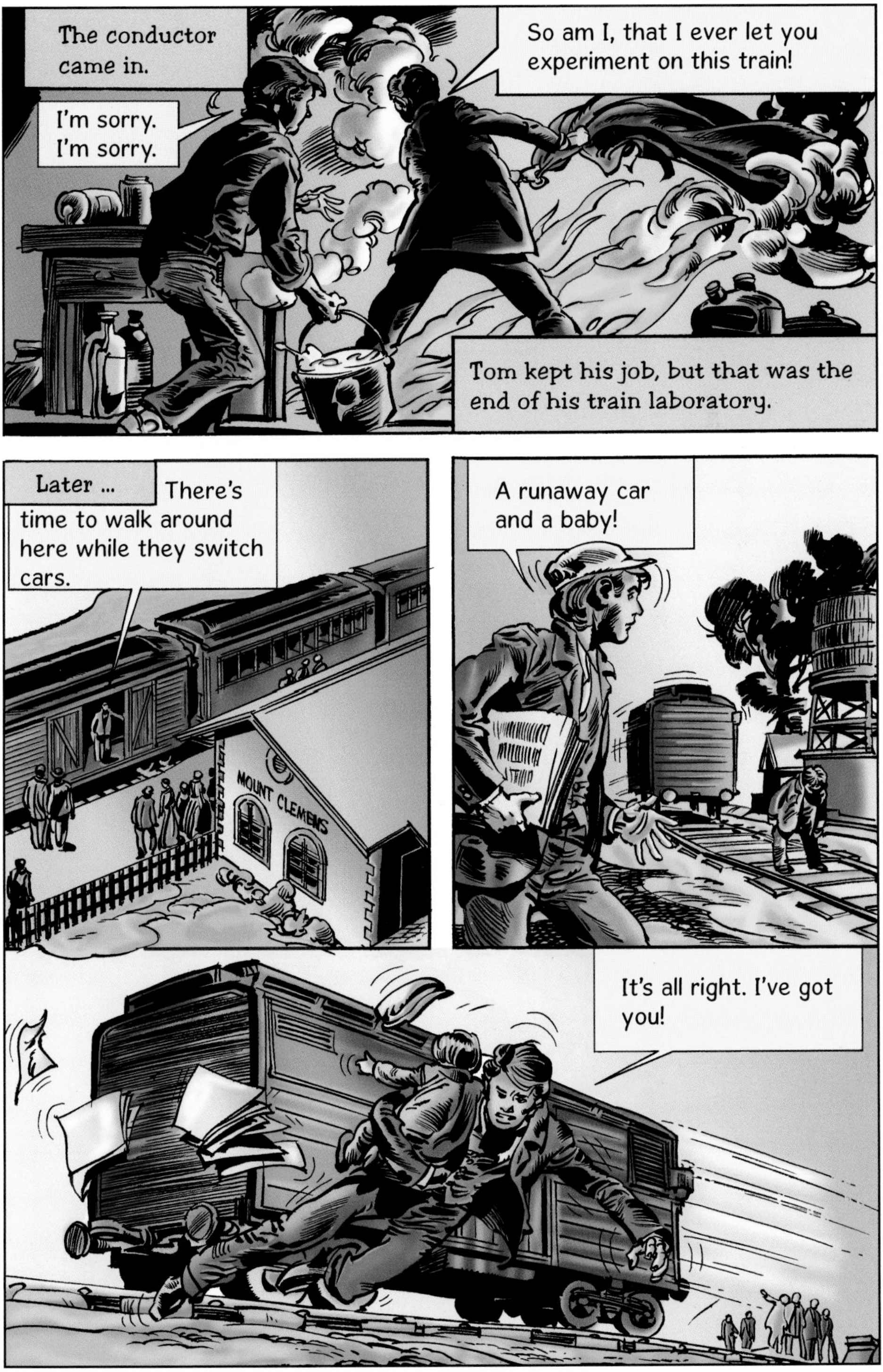
The conductor came in.
I'm sorry. I'm sorry.
So am I, that I ever let you experiment on this train!
Tom kept his job, but that was the end of his train laboratory.
Later ...
There's time to walk around here while they switch cars.
MOUNT CLEMENS
A runaway car and a baby!
It's all right. I've got you!

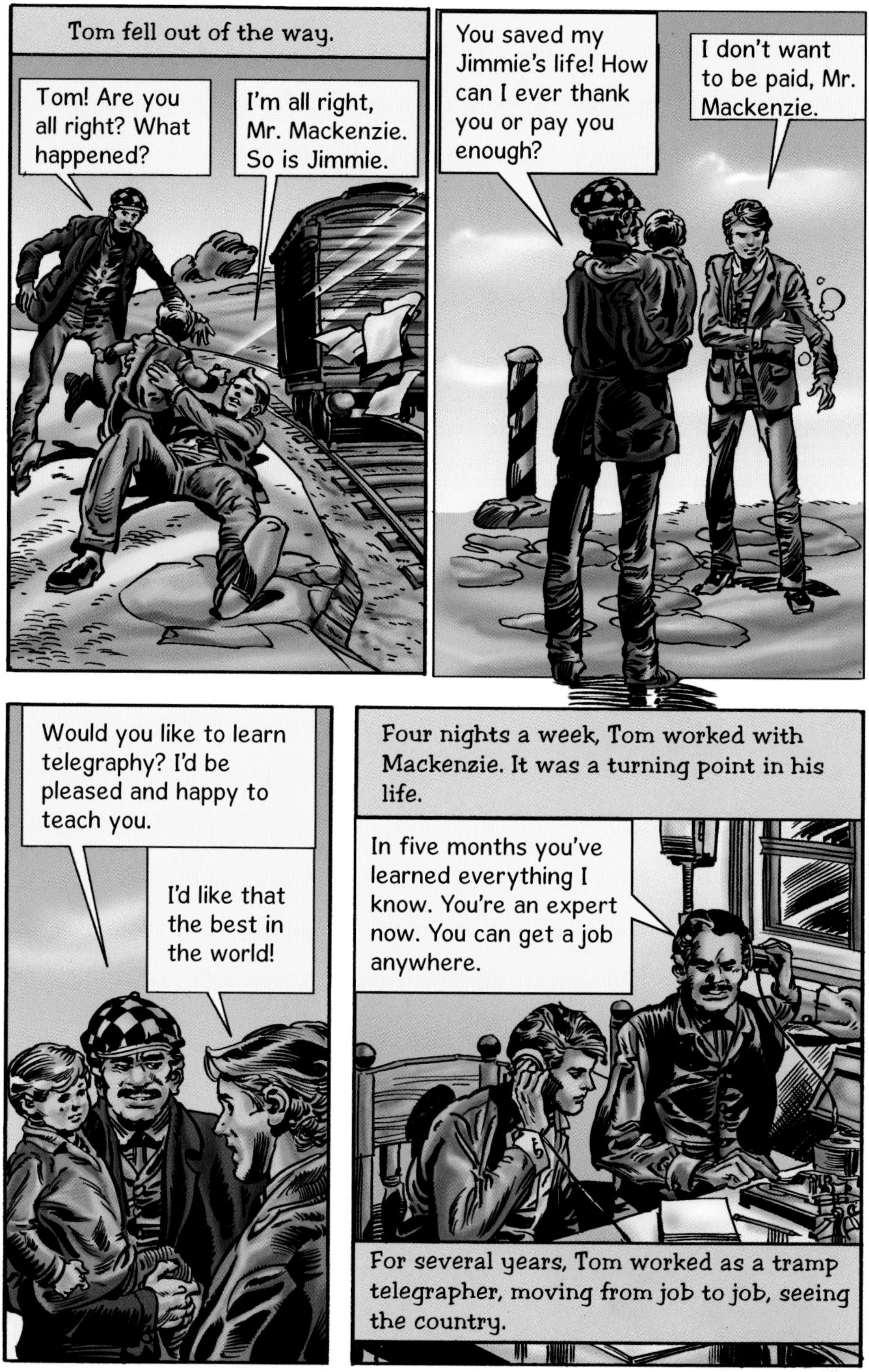
Tom fell out of the way.
Tom! Are you all right? What happened?
I'm all right, Mr. Mackenzie. So is Jimmie.
You saved my Jimmie's life! How can I ever thank you or pay you enough?
I don't want to be paid, Mr. Mackenzie.
Would you like to learn telegraphy? I'd be pleased and happy to teach you.
I'd like that the best in the world!
Four nights a week, Tom worked with Mackenzie. It was a turning point in his life.
In five months you've learned everything I know. You're an expert now. You can get a job anywhere.
For several years, Tom worked as a tramp telegrapher, moving from job to job, seeing the country.

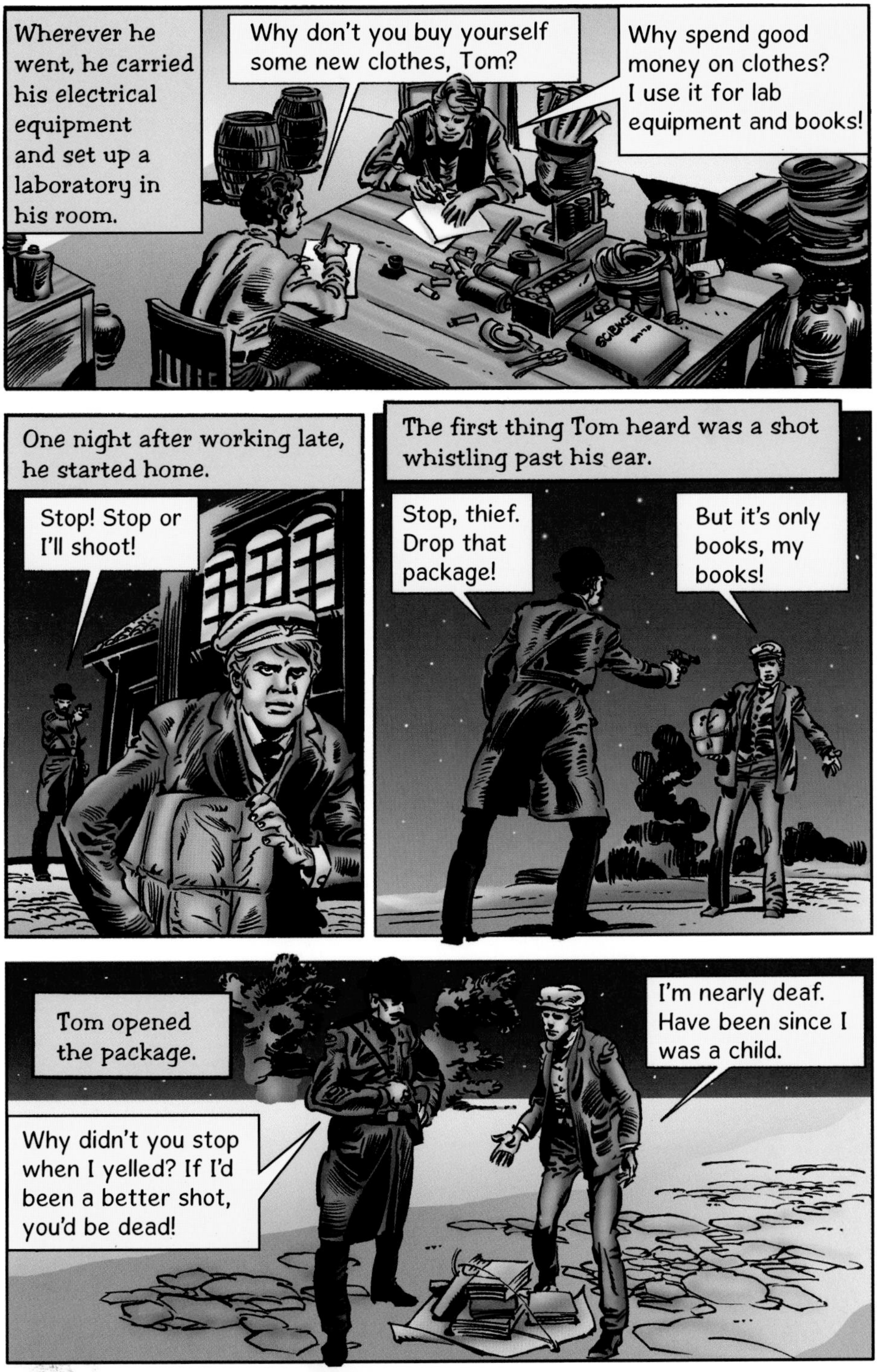
Wherever he went, he carried his electrical equipment and set up a laboratory in his room.
Why don't you buy yourself some new clothes, Tom?
Why spend good money on clothes? I use it for lab equipment and books!
SCIENCE
One night after working late, he started home.
Stop! Stop or I'll shoot!
The first thing Tom heard was a shot whistling past his ear.
Stop, thief. Drop that package!
But it's only books, my books!
Tom opened the package.
I'm nearly deaf. Have been since I was a child.
Why didn't you stop when I yelled? If I'd been a better shot, you'd be dead!

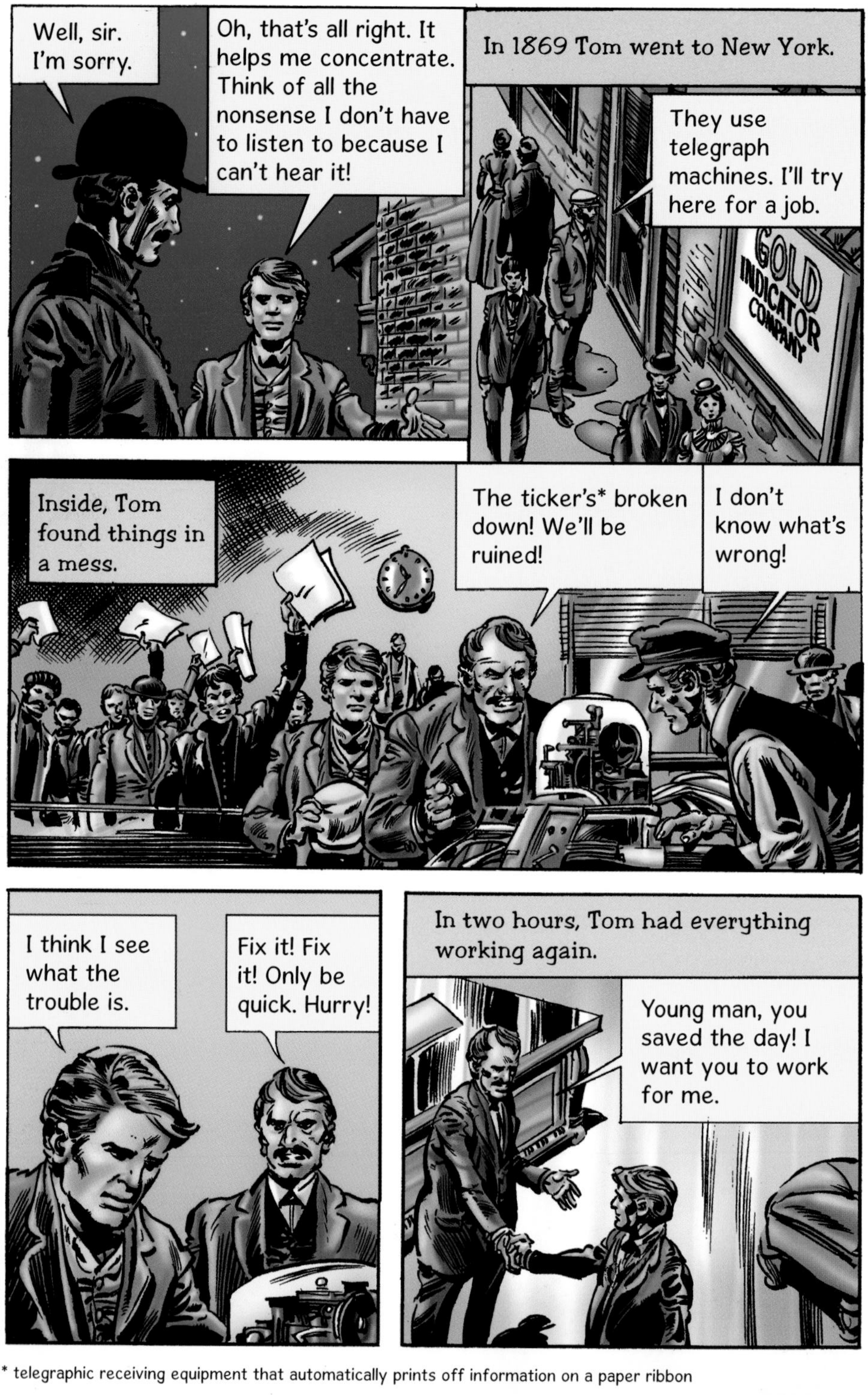
Well, sir. I'm sorry.
Oh, that's all right. It helps me concentrate. Think of all the nonsense I don't have to listen to because I can't hear it!
In 1869 Tom went to New York.
They use telegraph machines. I'll try here for a job.
GOLD INDICATOR COMPANY
Inside, Tom found things in a mess.
The ticker's* broken down! We'll be ruined!
I don't know what's wrong!
I think I see what the trouble is.
Fix it! Fix it! Only be quick. Hurry!
In two hours, Tom had everything working again.
Young man, you saved the day! I want you to work for me.

* telegraphic receiving equipment that automatically prints off information on a paper ribbon

Tom had a good job and a high salary. But he stayed only two months.

I'm sorry, but I have so many ideas. I want to work on my inventions.

First, he made an improved stock ticker.

I'm going to show it to the Gold and Stock Telegraphy Company. I'll ask $5,000 for it, but I'll take $3,000.

Tom demonstrated his device.

Well, young man, what will you take for it?

Uh, make me an offer.

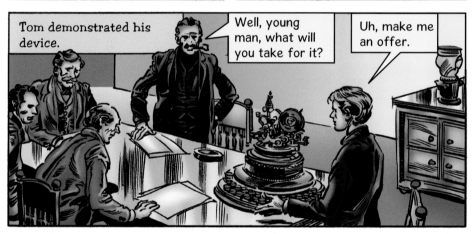

How does forty thousand dollars strike you?

Uh, forty thou ... I'll take it!

Tom agreed to manufacture the new stock tickers. In thirty days, he had spent the $40,000 renting space and setting up a machine shop and laboratory in Newark, New Jersey.

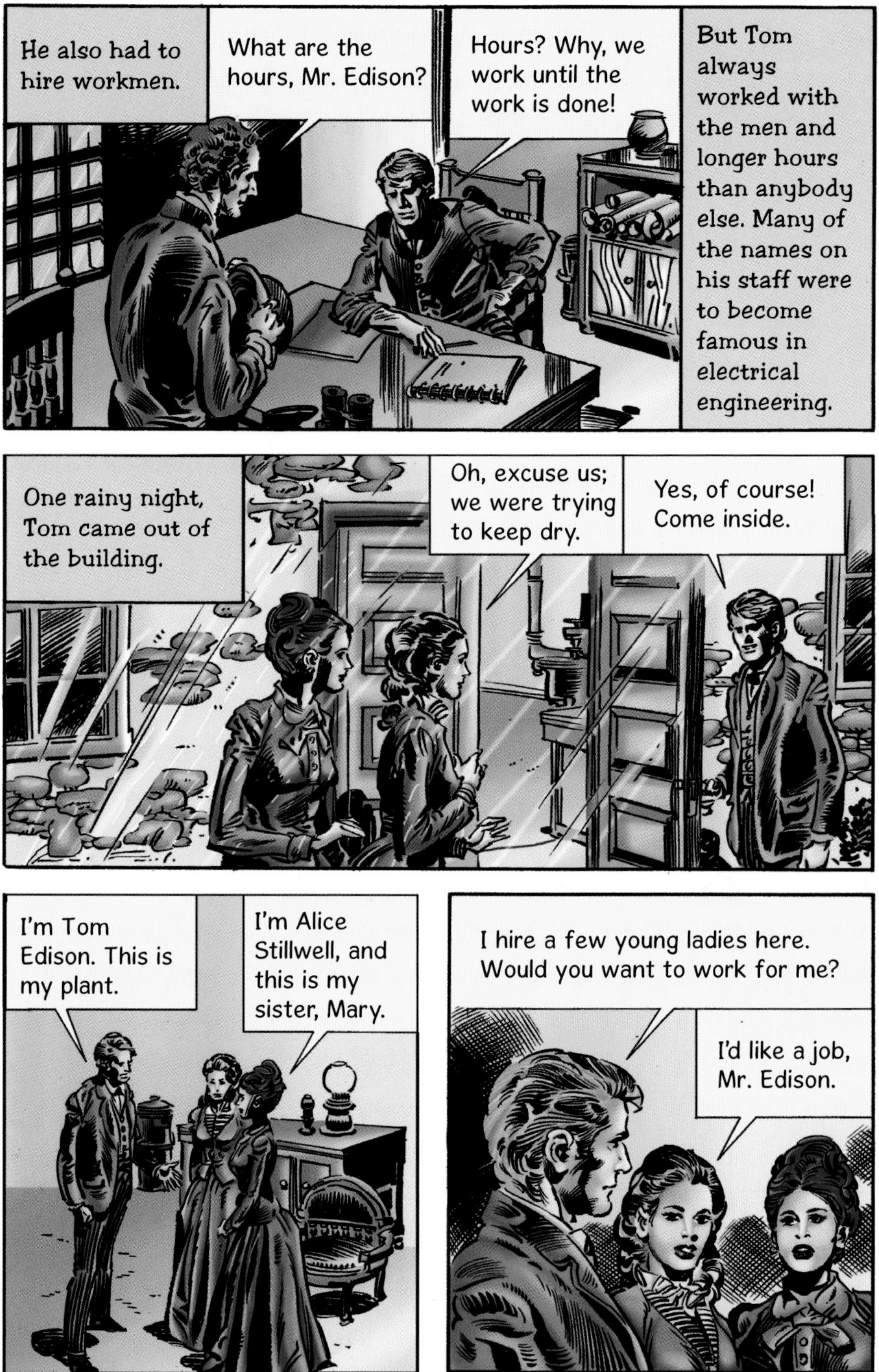
He also had to hire workmen.
What are the hours, Mr. Edison?
Hours? Why, we work until the work is done!
But Tom always worked with the men and longer hours than anybody else. Many of the names on his staff were to become famous in electrical engineering.
One rainy night, Tom came out of the building.
Oh, excuse us; we were trying to keep dry.
Yes, of course! Come inside.
I'm Tom Edison. This is my plant.
I'm Alice Stillwell, and this is my sister, Mary.
I hire a few young ladies here. Would you want to work for me?
I'd like a job, Mr. Edison.

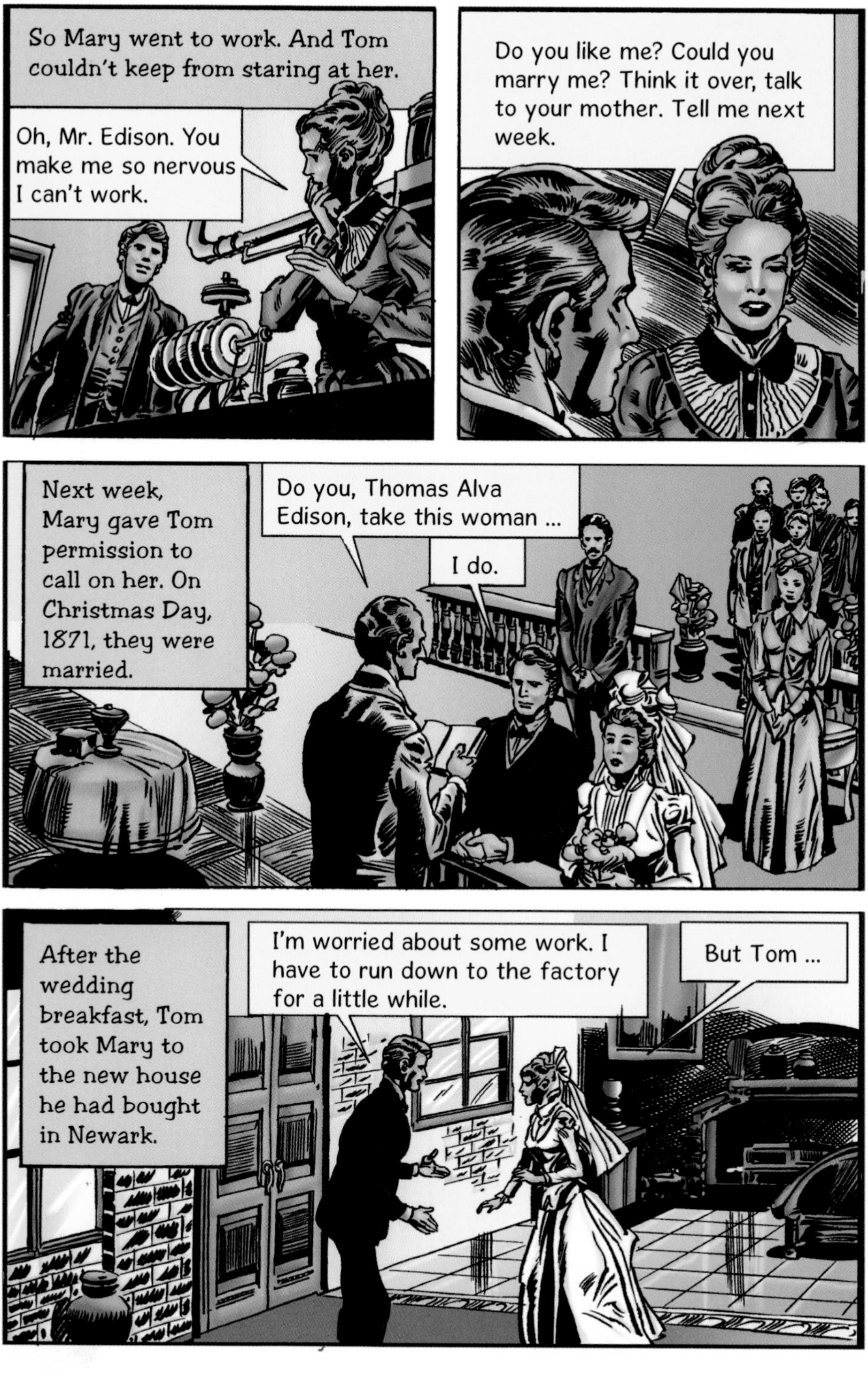
So Mary went to work. And Tom couldn't keep from staring at her.
Oh, Mr. Edison. You make me so nervous I can't work.
Do you like me? Could you marry me? Think it over, talk to your mother. Tell me next week.
Next week, Mary gave Tom permission to call on her. On Christmas Day, 1871, they were married.
Do you, Thomas Alva Edison, take this woman ...
I do.
After the wedding breakfast, Tom took Mary to the new house he had bought in Newark.
I'm worried about some work. I have to run down to the factory for a little while.
But Tom ...

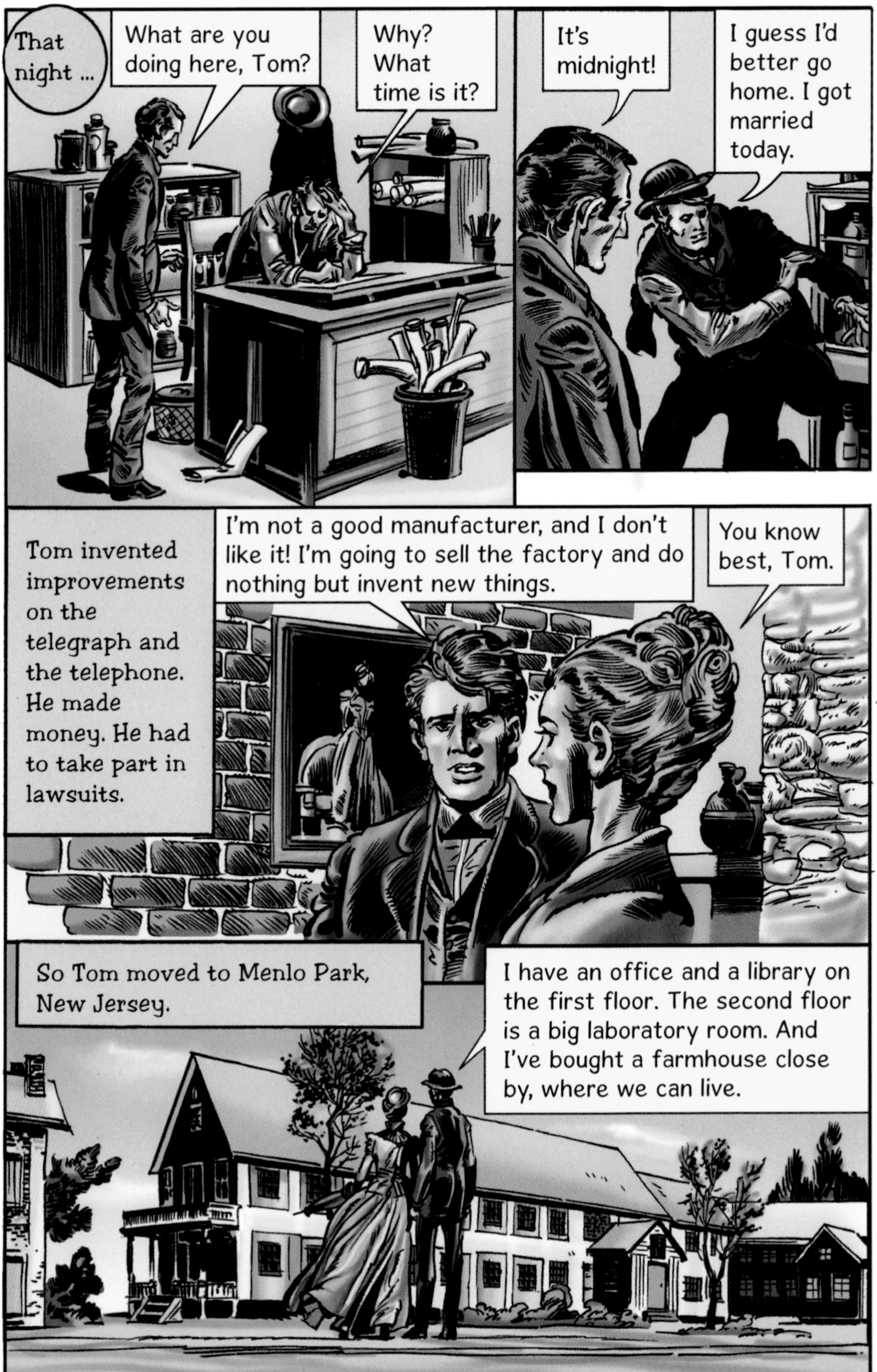

That night ...
What are you doing here, Tom?
Why? What time is it?
It's midnight!
I guess I'd better go home. I got married today.
Tom invented improvements on the telegraph and the telephone. He made money. He had to take part in lawsuits.
I'm not a good manufacturer, and I don't like it! I'm going to sell the factory and do nothing but invent new things.
You know best, Tom.
So Tom moved to Menlo Park, New Jersey.
I have an office and a library on the first floor. The second floor is a big laboratory room. And I've bought a farmhouse close by, where we can live.

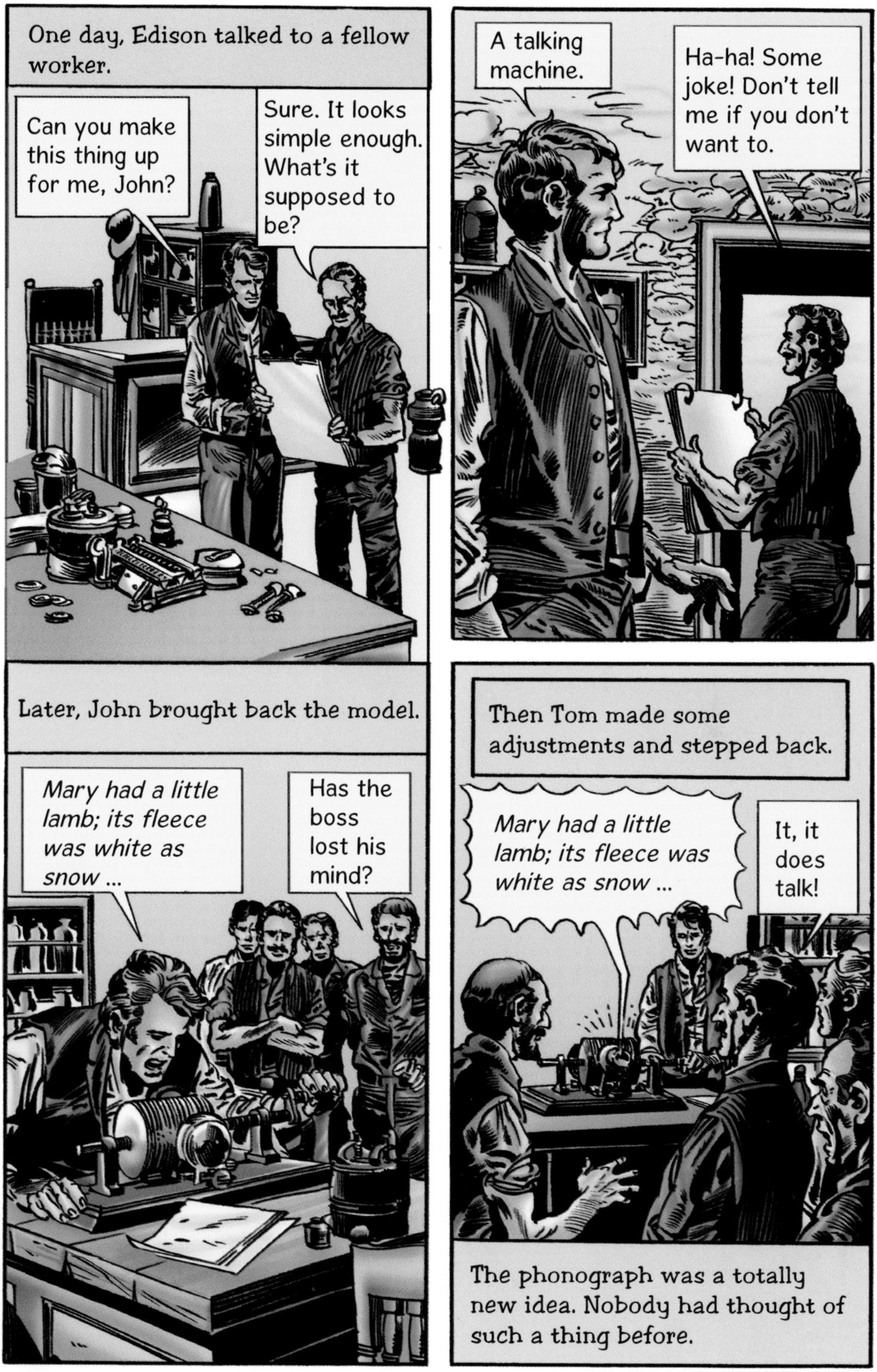
One day, Edison talked to a fellow worker.
Can you make this thing up for me, John?
Sure. It looks simple enough. What's it supposed to be?
A talking machine.
Ha-ha! Some joke! Don't tell me if you don't want to.
Later, John brought back the model.
Mary had a little lamb; its fleece was white as snow ...
Has the boss lost his mind?
Then Tom made some adjustments and stepped back.
Mary had a little lamb; its fleece was white as snow ...
It, it does talk!
The phonograph was a totally new idea. Nobody had thought of such a thing before.

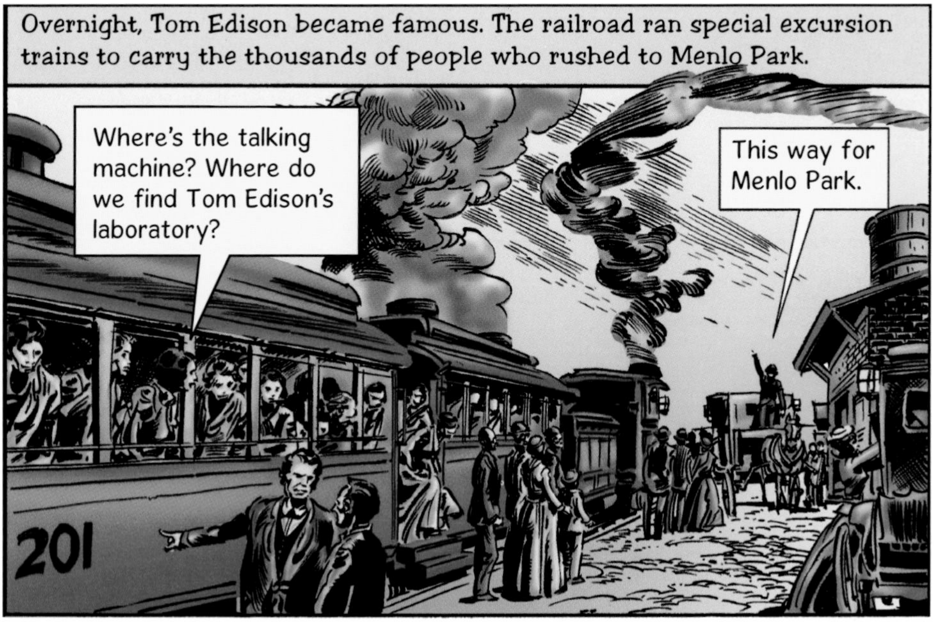
Overnight, Tom Edison became famous. The railroad ran special excursion trains to carry the thousands of people who rushed to Menlo Park.
Where's the talking machine? Where do we find Tom Edison's laboratory?
This way for Menlo Park.
201

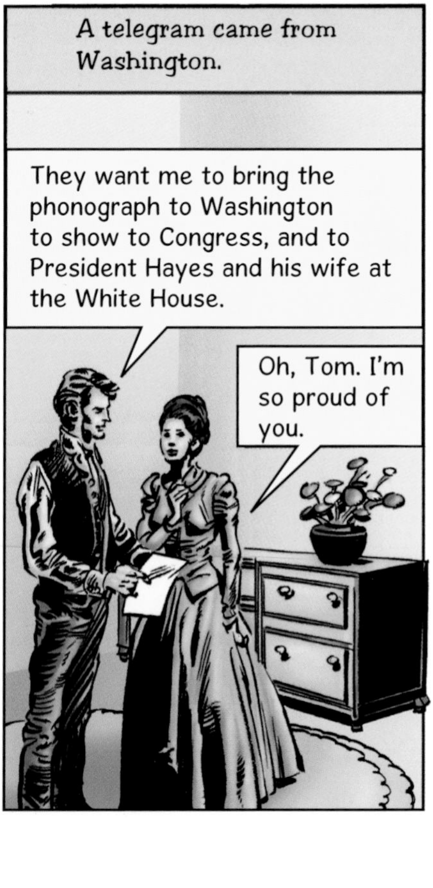
A telegram came from Washington.
They want me to bring the phonograph to Washington to show to Congress, and to President Hayes and his wife at the White House.
Oh, Tom. I'm so proud of you.

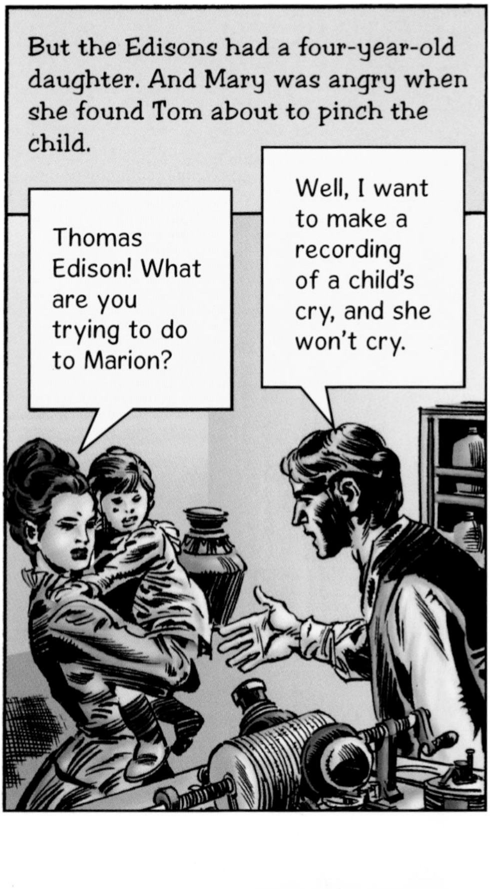
But the Edisons had a four-year-old daughter. And Mary was angry when she found Tom about to pinch the child.
Thomas Edison! What are you trying to do to Marion?
Well, I want to make a recording of a child's cry, and she won't cry.

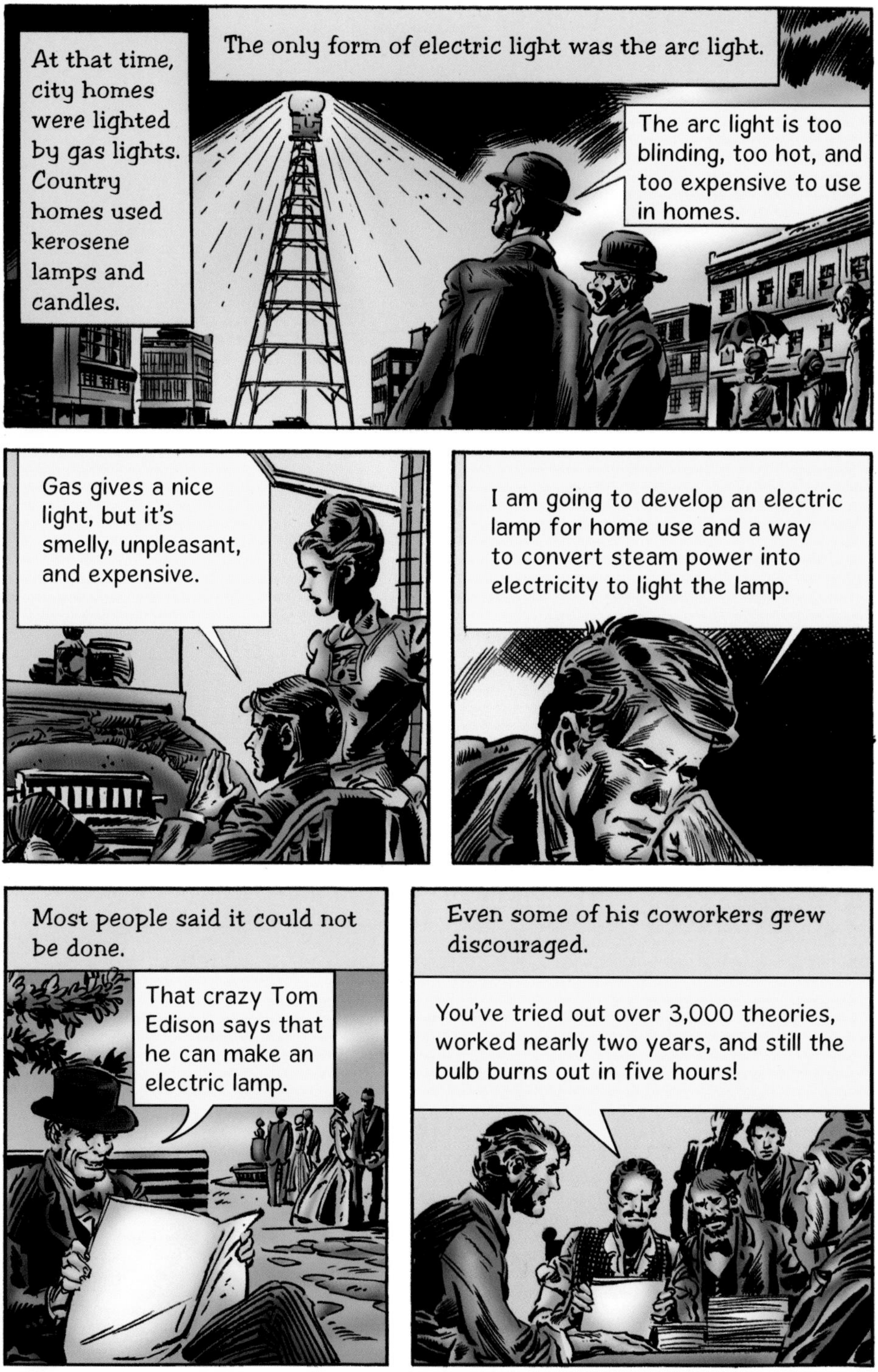
At that time, city homes were lighted by gas lights. Country homes used kerosene lamps and candles.
The only form of electric light was the arc light.
The arc light is too blinding, too hot, and too expensive to use in homes.
Gas gives a nice light, but it's smelly, unpleasant, and expensive.
I am going to develop an electric lamp for home use and a way to convert steam power into electricity to light the lamp.
Most people said it could not be done.
That crazy Tom Edison says that he can make an electric lamp.
Even some of his coworkers grew discouraged.
You've tried out over 3,000 theories, worked nearly two years, and still the bulb burns out in five hours!

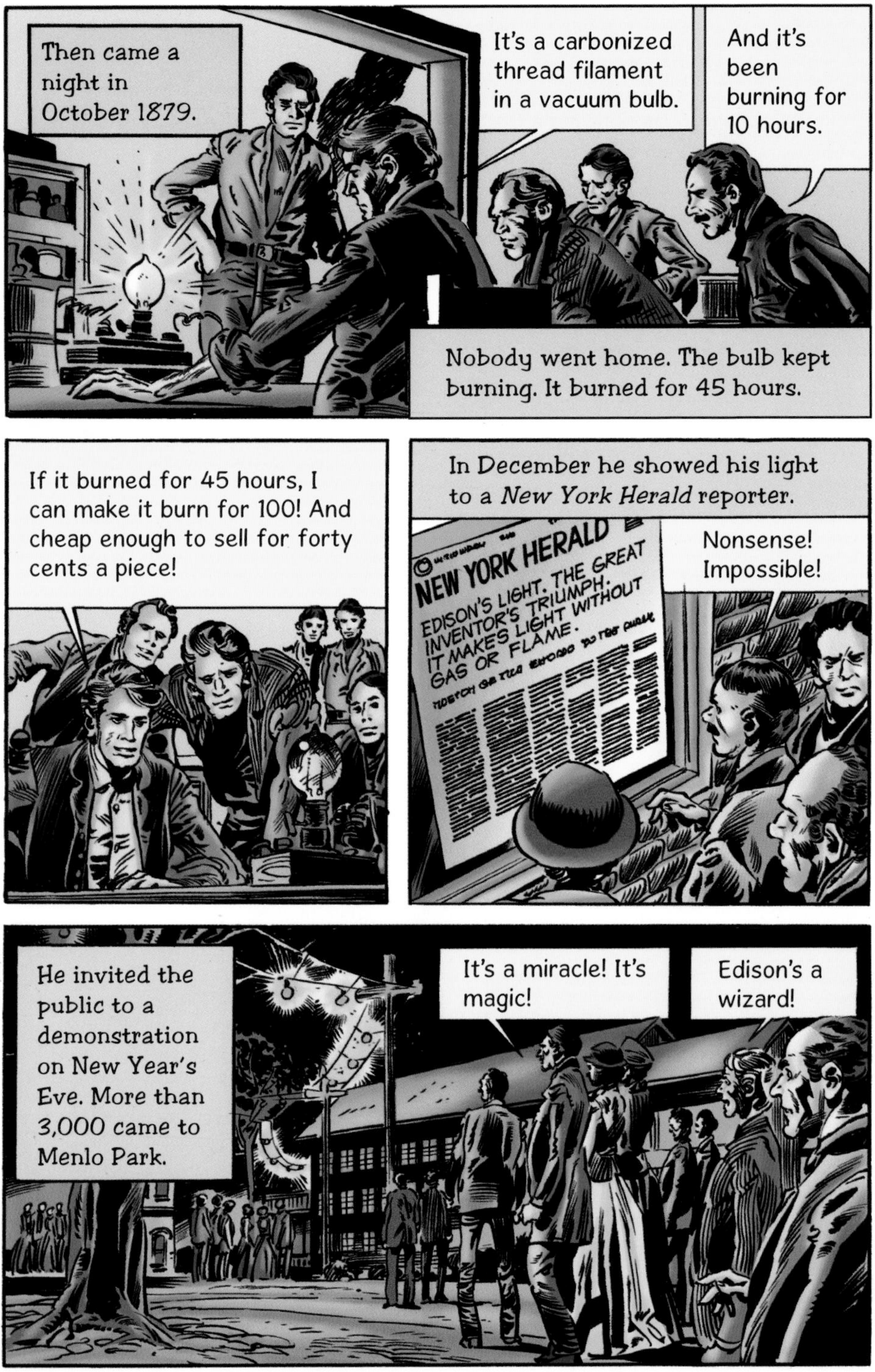
Then came a night in October 1879.
It's a carbonized thread filament in a vacuum bulb.
And it's been burning for 10 hours.
Nobody went home. The bulb kept burning. It burned for 45 hours.
If it burned for 45 hours, I can make it burn for 100! And cheap enough to sell for forty cents a piece!
In December he showed his light to a *New York Herald* reporter.
NEW YORK HERALD
EDISON'S LIGHT. THE GREAT INVENTOR'S TRIUMPH. IT MAKES LIGHT WITHOUT GAS OR FLAME.
Nonsense! Impossible!
He invited the public to a demonstration on New Year's Eve. More than 3,000 came to Menlo Park.
It's a miracle! It's magic!
Edison's a wizard!

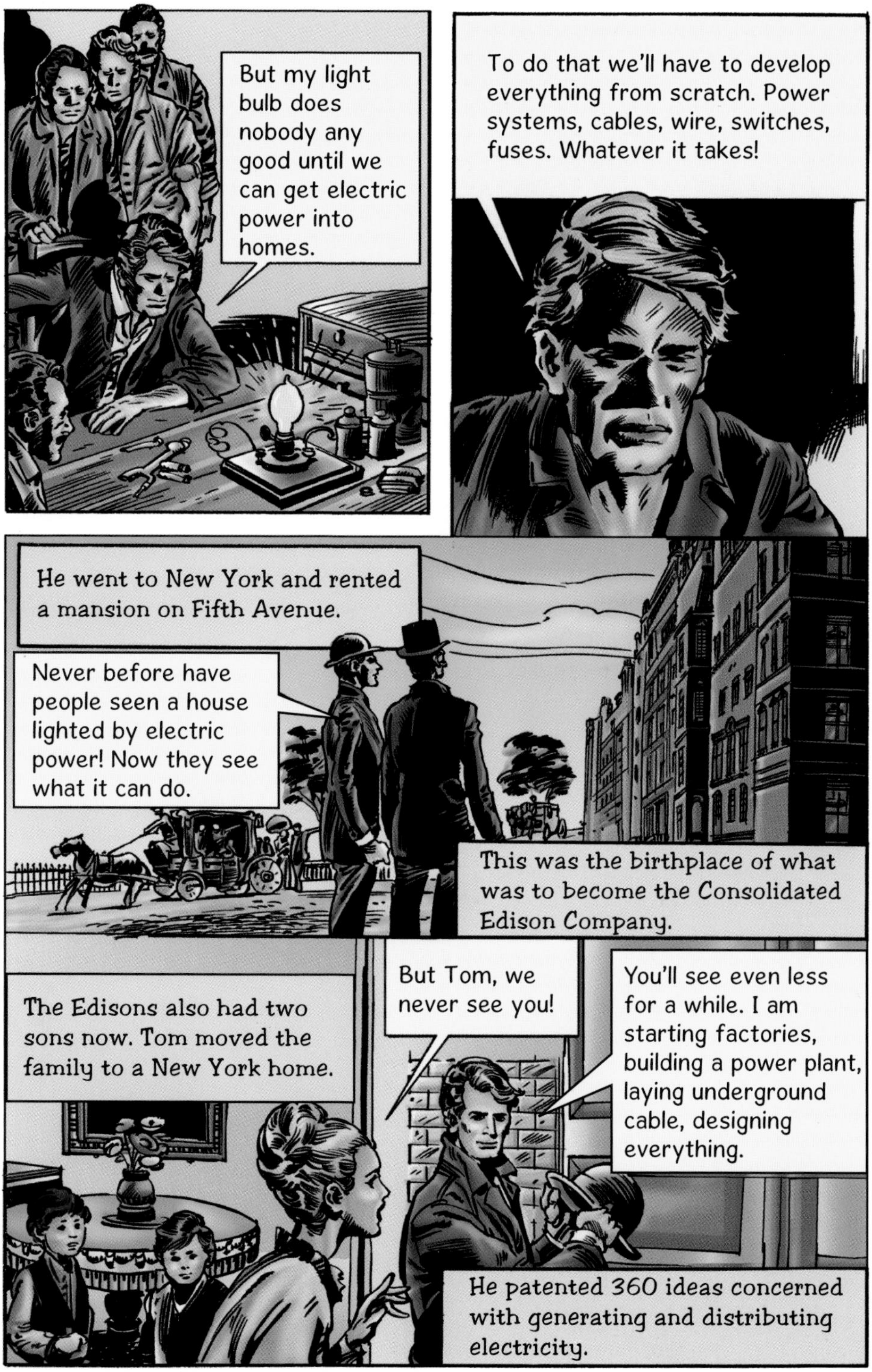
But my light bulb does nobody any good until we can get electric power into homes.
To do that we'll have to develop everything from scratch. Power systems, cables, wire, switches, fuses. Whatever it takes!
He went to New York and rented a mansion on Fifth Avenue.
Never before have people seen a house lighted by electric power! Now they see what it can do.
This was the birthplace of what was to become the Consolidated Edison Company.
The Edisons also had two sons now. Tom moved the family to a New York home.
But Tom, we never see you!
You'll see even less for a while. I am starting factories, building a power plant, laying underground cable, designing everything.
He patented 360 ideas concerned with generating and distributing electricity.

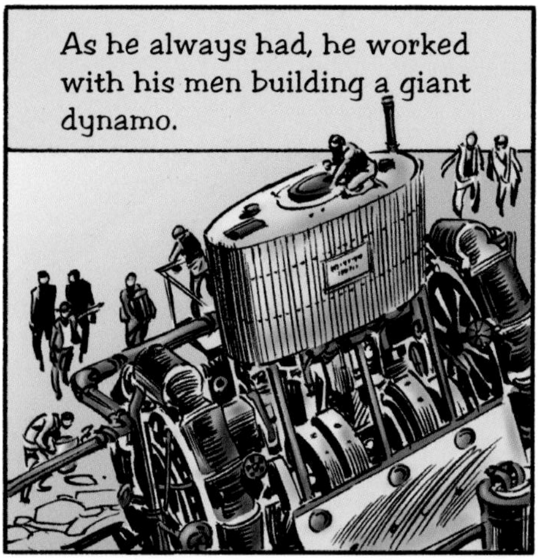
As he always had, he worked with his men building a giant dynamo.

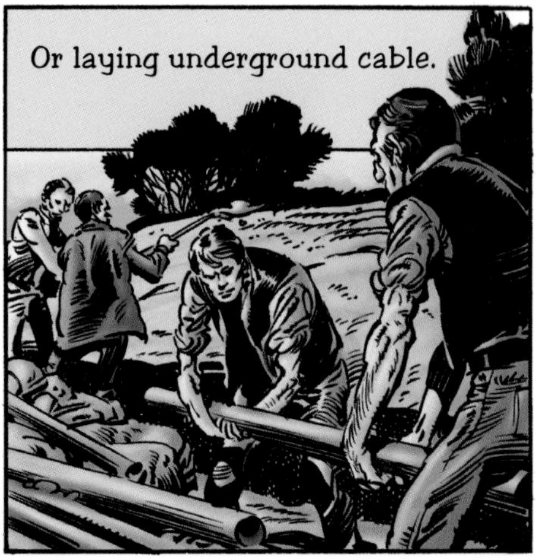
Or laying underground cable.

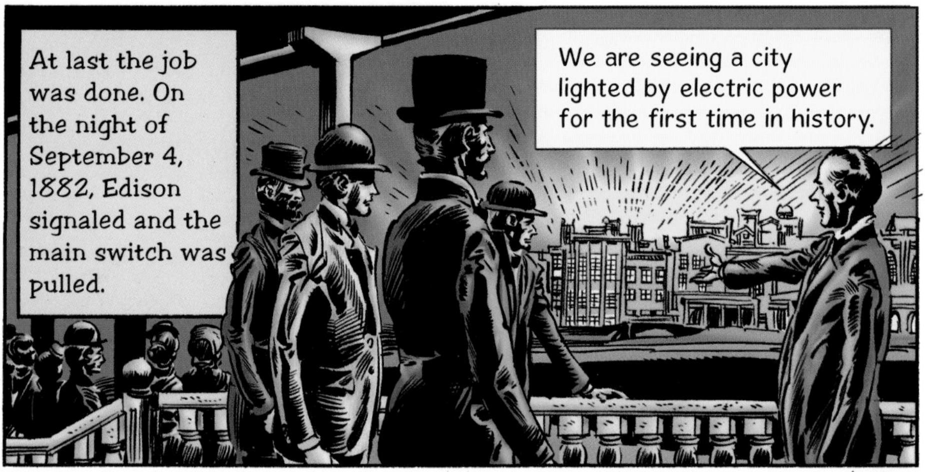
At last the job was done. On the night of September 4, 1882, Edison signaled and the main switch was pulled.
We are seeing a city lighted by electric power for the first time in history.

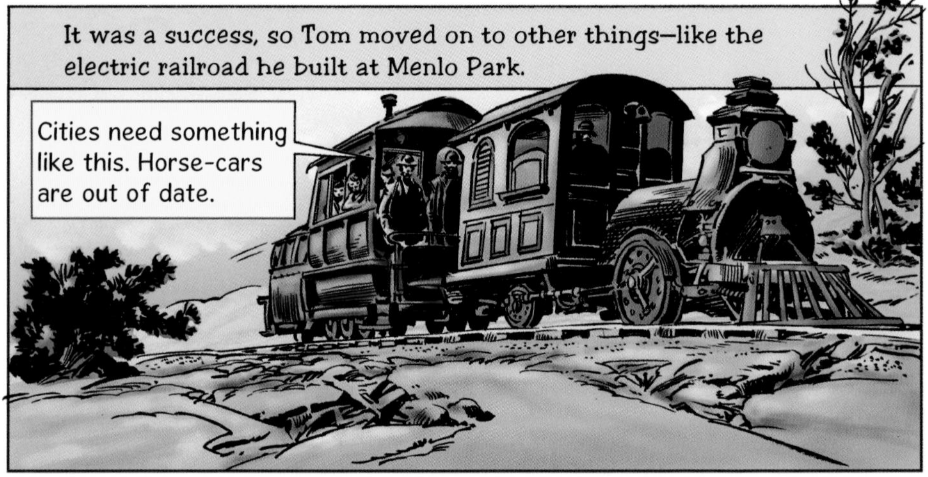
It was a success, so Tom moved on to other things—like the electric railroad he built at Menlo Park.
Cities need something like this. Horse-cars are out of date.

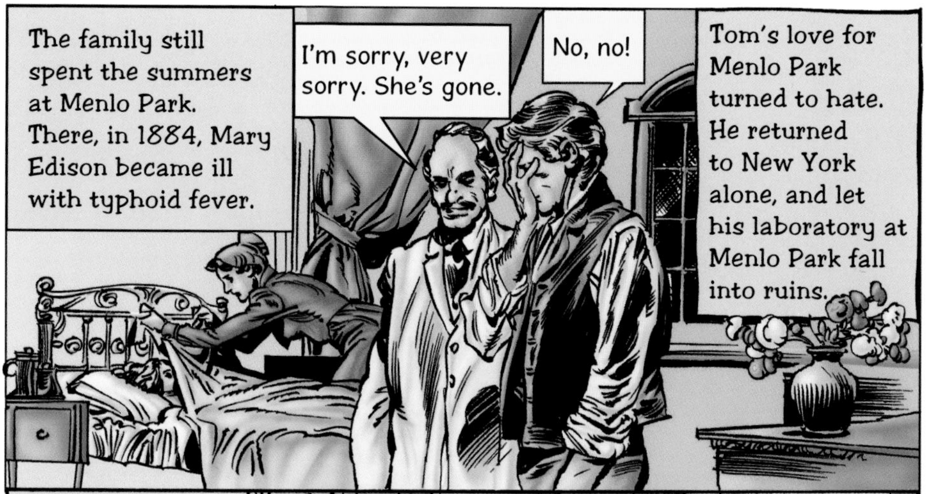
The family still spent the summers at Menlo Park. There, in 1884, Mary Edison became ill with typhoid fever.
I'm sorry, very sorry. She's gone.
No, no!
Tom's love for Menlo Park turned to hate. He returned to New York alone, and let his laboratory at Menlo Park fall into ruins.

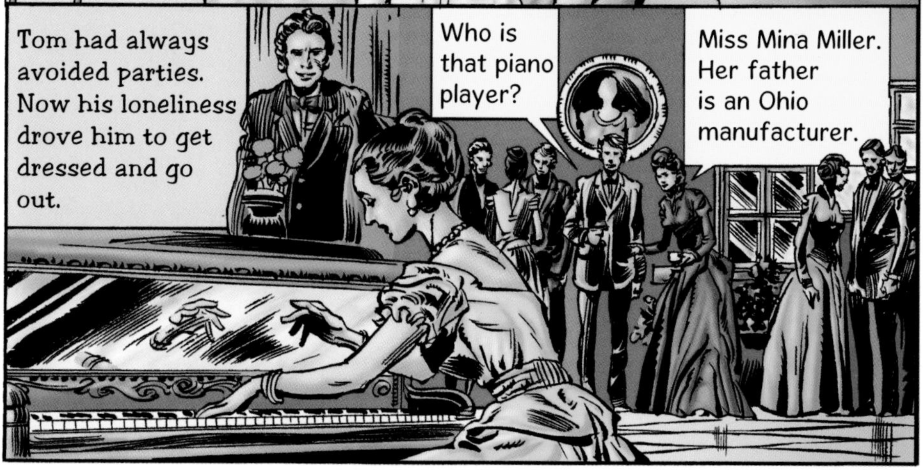
Tom had always avoided parties. Now his loneliness drove him to get dressed and go out.
Who is that piano player?
Miss Mina Miller. Her father is an Ohio manufacturer.

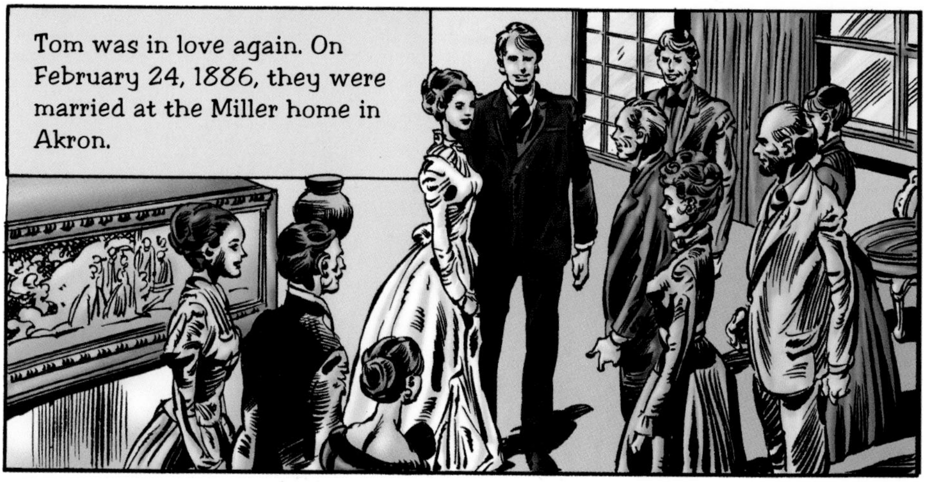
Tom was in love again. On February 24, 1886, they were married at the Miller home in Akron.

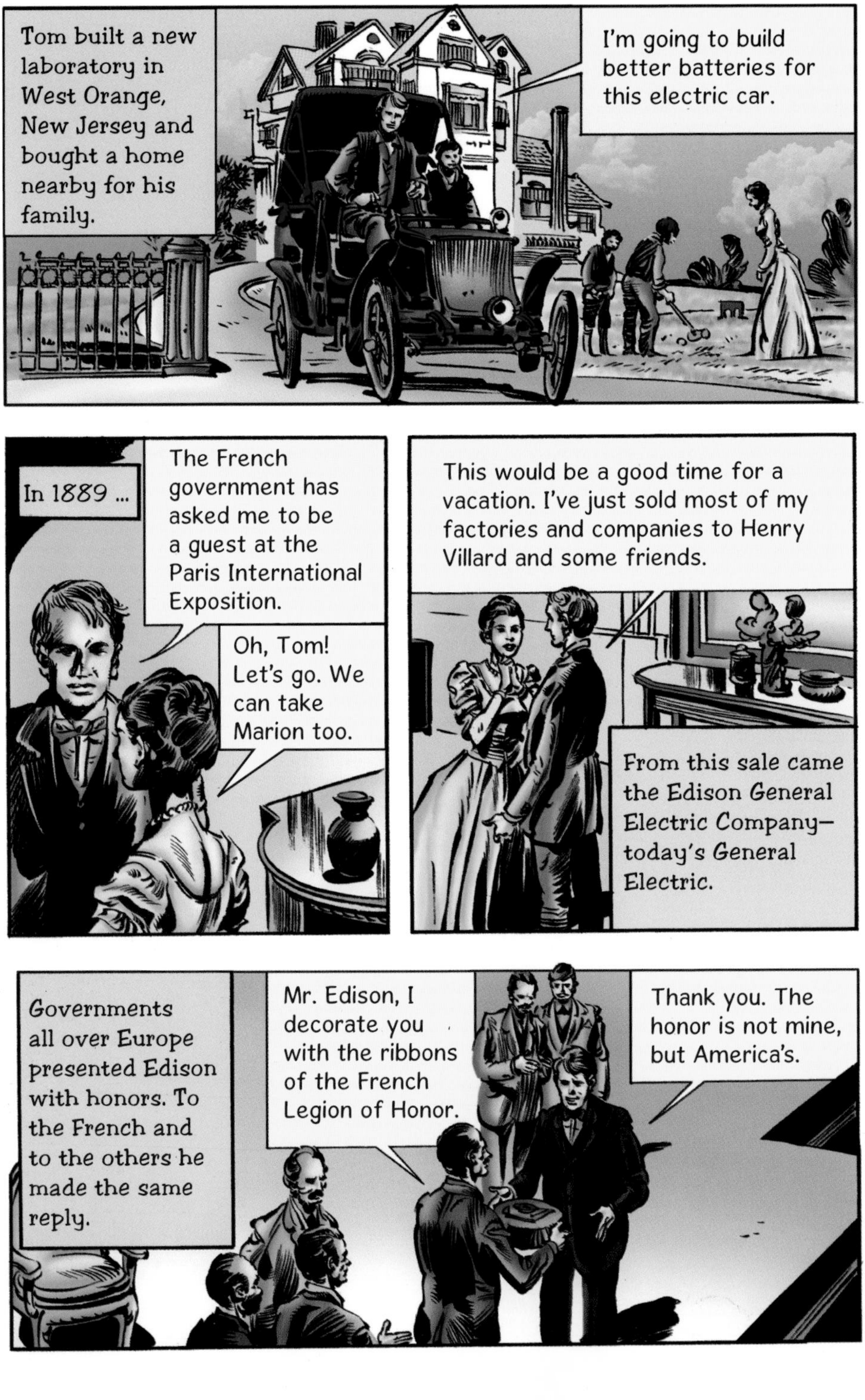
Tom built a new laboratory in West Orange, New Jersey and bought a home nearby for his family.
I'm going to build better batteries for this electric car.
In 1889 ...
The French government has asked me to be a guest at the Paris International Exposition.
Oh, Tom! Let's go. We can take Marion too.
This would be a good time for a vacation. I've just sold most of my factories and companies to Henry Villard and some friends.
From this sale came the Edison General Electric Company— today's General Electric.
Governments all over Europe presented Edison with honors. To the French and to the others he made the same reply.
Mr. Edison, I decorate you with the ribbons of the French Legion of Honor.
Thank you. The honor is not mine, but America's.

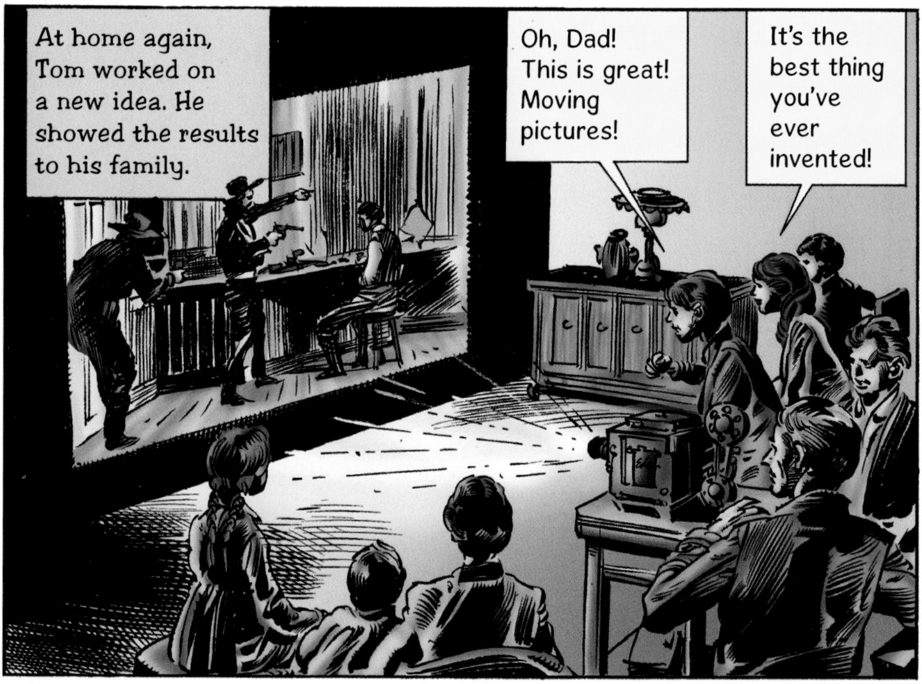
At home again, Tom worked on a new idea. He showed the results to his family.
Oh, Dad! This is great! Moving pictures!
It's the best thing you've ever invented!

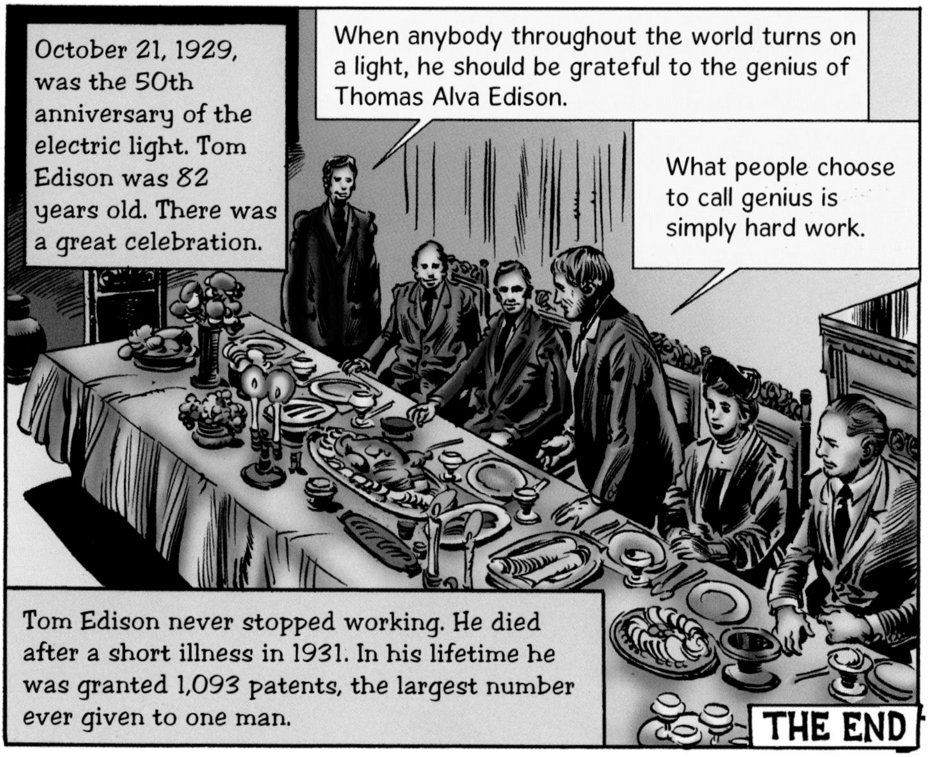
October 21, 1929, was the 50th anniversary of the electric light. Tom Edison was 82 years old. There was a great celebration.
When anybody throughout the world turns on a light, he should be grateful to the genius of Thomas Alva Edison.
What people choose to call genius is simply hard work.
Tom Edison never stopped working. He died after a short illness in 1931. In his lifetime he was granted 1,093 patents, the largest number ever given to one man.
THE END

Saddleback's Graphic Fiction & Nonfiction

If you enjoyed this Graphic Biography ... you will also enjoy our other graphic titles including:

Graphic Classics

- Around the World in Eighty Days
- The Best of Poe
- Black Beauty
- The Call of the Wild
- A Christmas Carol
- A Connecticut Yankee in King Arthur's Court
- Dr. Jekyll and Mr. Hyde
- Dracula
- Frankenstein
- The Great Adventures of
- Sherlock Holmes
- Gulliver's Travels
- Huckleberry Finn
- The Hunchback of Notre Dame
- The Invisible Man
- Jane Eyre
- Journey to the Center of the Earth
- Kidnapped
- The Last of the Mohicans
- The Man in the Iron Mask
- Moby Dick
- The Mutiny On Board H.M.S. Bounty
- The Mysterious Island
- The Prince and the Pauper
- The Red Badge of Courage
- The Scarlet Letter
- The Swiss Family Robinson
- A Tale of Two Cities
- The Three Musketeers
- The Time Machine
- Tom Sawyer
- Treasure Island
- 20,000 Leagues Under the Sea
- The War of the Worlds

Graphic Shakespeare

- As You Like It
- Hamlet
- Julius Caesar
- King Lear
- Macbeth
- The Merchant of Venice
- A Midsummer Night's Dream
- Othello
- Romeo and Juliet
- The Taming of the Shrew
- The Tempest
- Twelfth Night

SADDLEBACK
EDUCATIONAL PUBLISHING

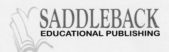